Is That Rain?

Explorer Challenge

What is drinking from the puddle?

OXFORD
UNIVERSITY PRESS

Mum was setting off for the
market with Biff and Kipper.

"Shall I get my raincoat?"
said Biff. "It might rain."

"I will check the weather for you," said Dad.

"It will be hot with lots of sun!" he said.

"We will not need an umbrella then," said Mum.

At the market, Kipper said, "I can
feel drops of rain."

The rain fell harder and harder.
"Oh no!" said Biff.

They had to shelter at the market
and wait.

"The rain is getting a bit lighter!"
said Biff.

"Quick!" said Mum. "We can run to that shop!"

"Ow!" said Kipper.
"This rain hurts!"

"It is not rain now," said Biff.
"This is *hail!*"

They had to shelter until the end of the bad weather.

At home, Dad said, "How was
the market?"
"We had hail!" said Kipper.

"And rain!" said Biff.
"We got soaking wet!" said Mum.

"Oops," said Dad. "I was looking at the weather for a different town!"

Retell the Story

Look at the pictures and retell the story in your own words.

Look Back, Explorers

Where were Mum, Biff and Kipper going?

Where did they shelter from the rain?

Why did Dad say it was going to be hot and sunny?

Did you find out what was drinking from the puddle?

What's Next, Explorers?

Now read about what happens when it rains and why rain is good ...

Rain!

Becca Heddle

Series created by Roderick Hunt and Alex Brychta

OXFORD

Explorer Challenge
for *Rain!*

What is drinking from the river?